Getaway Girl

Terry Ann Thaxton

SALT

LONDON

PUBLISHED BY SALT PUBLISHING
Dutch House, 307–308 High Holborn, London WC1V 7LL United Kingdom

© Terry Ann Thaxton, 2011

Salt Publishing 2011

Printed and bound in the United States by Lightning Source Inc

Typeset in Swift 9.5 / 13

ISBN 978 1 84471 511 4 paperback

1 3 5 7 9 8 6 4 2

Getaway Girl

TERRY ANN THAXTON has published poetry in *Cimarron Review, Connecticut Review, Hawai'i Review, Hayden's Ferry, West Branch,* and other journals. She is Associate Professor of English at the University of Central Florida in Orlando, where she teaches creative writing and directs The Literary Arts Partnership.

Contents

Acknowledgements

Grateful acknowledgment is made to the following publications where some of these poems first appeared, sometimes in different versions:

anderbo.com, Ascent, Borderlands: Texas Poetry Review, Cimarron Review, Comstock Review, Concho River, The Florida Review, Flyway, Foliate Oak, Forge, Hawaii Review, Hollins Critic, Lullwater, Organization & Environment, Paintbrush, Potomac Review, Santa Fe Literary Review, The Southeast Review, Sou'wester, Sow's Ear, SunDog: The Southeast Review, Tampa Review, West Branch.

I would like to thank the University of Central Florida and the Atlantic Center for the Arts for space and time to work on these poems. Heartfelt thanks to Kelle Groom, Judith Hemschemeyer, Russ Kesler, Pat Rushin, and John Schell for their early and continued support and encouragement. Many thanks to David Rivard, Mary Ruefle, Leslie Ullman, David Wojahn, and Don Stap for their help in shaping many of these poems.

Special thanks to my son, Adam.

"I suppose their little bones have years ago been lost among the stones and winds of those high glacial pastures. I suppose their feathers blew eventually into the piles of tumbleweed beneath the straggling cattle fences and rotted there in the mountain snows, along with dead steers and all the other things that drift to an end in the corners of the wire.... It is a funny thing what the brain will do with memories and how it will treasure them and finally bring them into odd juxtapositions with other things, as though it wanted to make a design, or get some meaning out of them, whether you want it or not, or even see it."

—LOREN EISELEY, THE IMMENSE JOURNEY

I

Getaway Girl

Getaway Girl

Inside the house, red
as a bruised peach, someone
kicked me saying *this
is love*, but
I found my broken
perfume bottles at the edge
of the stone steps, my
clothes hanging
off branches,
and my only escape
was over homemade ball fields
where I found myself
chased by headlights
of the drunken car
he drove that made the baby
inside die. To remind me
of the baby,
he buried—under a pile
of old garbage bags—
the dog he shot. I put my hands
through the front
window to make him
stop, but every night, in my dreams,
I looked for the baby I lost, tearing dress
after dress out of the branches.
My black coat hid the face
I kept trying to lose. And when he left
to buy apologies
at the card shop
I hoped he would
not return. There were other
times I waited
for him, committed crimes
for him, like the time I kept
the motor running

in a truck at the edge
of a deserted road while he
rolled heavy electric spools
from construction sites,
carried stacks of lumber,
and then scattered
nails, hammers, and paint
into the truck bed. I was his
getaway girl. I remember
him urinating on me
as if I were a stone
statue by Picasso.
I wanted someone to take him
to Africa and lay him under
the heads of elephants.
I wanted to see him dead
in a lake of grass. Instead, he kept
pinning me against the wall,
tying me to the floor,
and I smelled the heat of Florida
coming up through
the tiles in the bathroom.
I begged my grandmother
to lift her arms from her grave,
grab his fists, his ankles
and tie him to the damp,
unforgiving earth.

The Yearning City

Married at eighteen, again
at twenty-one, I wore flowers and drifted
into parades. Once, to be with a man

I moved to Illinois, lived in his
house in the woods. I drove his jeep
on dirt roads until he realized I didn't do

laundry well, and he sent me away.
I emptied our savings, and took off
through the night for Florida. Then a preacher

who knew my mother's God
married me at twenty-five,
and quoted the Bible every night through dinner.

Waiting became my art. Suitcases fell
from the closet. Land sprouted
behind doors. Clocks
came out of hiding.

Now the men I left think I ache
without them. Let me demand

a vase as a sequel to myself.
Let me eat the doors of my dollhouse.
Let me sleep in a bell.

Suicide Boys

Motherhood entered as a forest of silence
and I tried to open windows for my son
a child of birds playing as if he were a flower in the yard.
He sang of opening the ocean and rain
died in the fire of his hand and then one
day I went to town with my boy
his words dangling from his smiles
lizards dancing from his ears and I heard a sea
of fences crying for him to come into a strange
yard where all the days are loud where the book of farm
animals I read to him once are torn and childhood
wanders into the sandbox of distance. So I had to learn
to eat from the book of hope since he would only
listen to the cloud of children's voices that crept
into the sky where the gatherer of men
waited. And my boy's backpack filled
with what he thought would be the answers:
bird shit and empty fish hooks
a lost game of checkers and other
boys of suicide. I thought of his baby clothes at the shore
of our hometown hovering over the wayward
songs of sea grapes. Even there I knew something would open
and my son would fall into it I knew his face
would converge with the water his arms would adorn
the lily pads the woods would ache for him
and he would want to sneak into the forest as
wind. One day my son will appear
on the branch outside my window
as a palm warbler. Outside there are women
clicking fingers to an ancient song:
when you no longer need me to feed you the dance
when your backpack empties of answers
when the flowers no longer sing to you
when you lay your childhood voice in the river...

The Garden

Pine tree limbs spill in shadows over my son
      as he sleeps, and he cries out. I go to him
           as in prayer, bending

like a sparrow's crumpled
      nest. A white grave rises
           in his eyes. From the dark unkempt

of my dress, I do not wish to see him leave,
      but out the window
           I imagine him walking into the street,

blond hair rising from his head. He puts
      his hands in the air and goes behind
           other houses and doorways,

the lost openings of my life. He seems
      to float through tiny rifts
           in the fence. I want him to remember me,

a mother slicing strawberries
      grown in the backyard, hammering
           the walls of her house, covering

the roof with shingles, opening
      the door. I want to remember him
           entombing a snake in the freezer

because he refused to bury anything, I want to
      resurrect his grandparents,
           offer him a mother bearing

small boxes of dried leaves
      and stories. I do not want to be
           a woman hiding in the seeds

of her past. The phone rings,
        a voice says, "Your son is masquerading
                in my garden." Falling backward,

I want to give birth again.
        Brooms and dustpans
                stand in the garage. I convince myself

I am a mother hoeing
        the past, eating the weather
                of my life, bean stalk of my father,

radish mouth of my mother. The day runs
        into the street. I see myself falling
                to the ground, my dress

crushing berries, mouth opening.

Mad Insects

Let go of the scattering sounds of other boys
crushing butterflies in the schoolyard, eating
grasshoppers, stepping on your fingers.

Reach into the ground, into the dirt of your infancy
and find your own answers—
the madness inside you may never die.

Remember the saying of the water-skimmer
whose mouth filled with mud water and dried fish.

Remember the soccer field when you were five,
the space you were told to stand in, the insects you found,
their antennae, thorax, heads, legs, abdomen.

Let go of what people say to you,
let go of their questions.

The echoes of the schoolyard may never stop
ringing in your sleep: the other children climbing monkey-bars,
shooting baskets, skipping rope, playing Red-Rover, Red-Rover.
Forget the straight lines other children make.

Your madness is almost invisible.

Remember the dragonfly behind you, the monarch above you,
the darkling beetle below you,
the harvester ant, the scarab, the ladybird.
Remember the insect-speak of your world that, even now,
calms you.

Take hold of the silence entering your world—
answer only the cries of the insects; your mother is not
leaving you and the insects in your dreams will never die,

they will not lie to you or drop
you into night. They will not ask you to explain
the words of the song you are singing.

A Different Life

when you leave your child under
twenty-four hour suicide watch
and he's eleven
and a prisoner in a private war

you blame yourself for the cars
he dove in front of
the buildings he jumped from
the wall of the bedroom
he banged his head on
the clothes you armed him with in the morning
the same clothes he shredded in the afternoon

you blame yourself for the time
you left him screaming
at the day care
and that woman washed his mouth out

you blame yourself for not knowing
how to do this
right

you walk out of the hospital
into an uncaring afternoon
and you reach for

what do you reach for?
the trees with leaves that fall apart?
the clouds that are really nothing?
the sun?

Boy in Distant Oak

The tree, empty of sunlight, his face
rough and awake, always awake

and the moon rising above
the house and into the black

floors, the faded demands
of a woman, asleep now, dreaming,

he's certain, of the bread crumbs
she wanted him

to see, the house, its walls, its dry
peelings, a puppy in low prayerful

utterings, but the mockingbird has not
yet begun his morning call —

somewhere there is a talking, untrained,
and after night is over, it leaves

as if it is water leaving, or a boy
in a distant

oak swinging up and then over, up and then
over the branches that clarify,

though the future is not able to see
what is about to happen: the gradual inclusion

of warblers, and like wings fluttering
above — no, under the emptiness of this space

between them, from the lighter
yellows into — nothing like a woodfire,

and not beyond the walls of the house,
an illusion of forest and lake where never

before, but always after the waking, the eyes
look for sunrise, unlike this, in her sleep

where she carries him bad water, but she
knows he will try not to remember this life

when, one day, he turns to her asleep,
and over her the blue moon is rising.

Night Ironing

Suppose the woman is barley draping the fields
and night happens often.
Suppose seven words can dry her tears
and children sing in a cloud
and morning coffee is enough.
God! Suppose she dies pruning grapes.
Suppose night ironing is common
and death drowns in dogwoods.
Suppose the woman is weary as an ass at dusk
whose work has brought her no water.
Suppose the wise masquerade as the moon
and it rains under boats.
Suppose the sun opens its flowers, empty and pale.

II

The God of the Dead

Good News

Some days meet that last bit of darkness
wagging their tails,
drooling toward the tart morning,

and in my yard: fat trees, and last night's
buried dreams. This morning

I am singing,
O I am in hell

in my own side yard, poisoning
the ants that turned a new gardenia bush into home,

the one I planted to honor my dead mother.
I refuse to sprinkle grits, like a neighbor once told

me, to kill the ants. What does it matter how they die?
White poison falls from their sky, and still

they dance to ten blooms.
Will their eyes swell? Are they not mute?

Already they're spreading the news: *we've been given a sign,*
a message from above; this is our sandy beach,

the one promised years ago.
They mistake my laughter for approval.

When they die, I mistake their leaving for a tapestry.
I make up stories about their lives.

I am the god of the dead.

Where Hell Is

—and there are days I do not want to swim
into my childhood, into the hayride from the church
parking lot to a drowsy park where darkness
came one Halloween night,
where out in the open Florida Southern Baptists
exchanged judgments. We were not allowed
to wear costumes, though, in secret, away from
the adults, we told ghost stories.
I already knew the Catholics were going to Hell.
I knew the joke was on them—
enthusiastic with their goodness.
I was with Beth. It was after she had slept with our
youth director, after our preacher told me not to
say things like that unless I had proof.
It was after her abortion, after our youth director was saved
from damnation. We outlived the ghosts
of Halloween again. The next year
we would not gather for even a hayride—
a new preacher warned of demons
and other followers of Satan. Instead we tried to save
the sick who were asleep in nursing homes. I rode
with Mr. Jones; we parked in a doctor's empty
lot and even then I knew that girls
were responsible for all the sins committed
by men and boys. In the distance, Halloween might be
Cinderella or a ballerina I could never become:
—stain on my dress, gnashing teeth in my hand,
and, in my mouth, forever and ever, a lake of fire.

Family Room

It is Saturday morning. Dad reclines
in his living room chair and Mom is still
in the kitchen just as she was last night
before I leaned against the window sill,
before Dad stroked my brother Ray's ear.
And after the first hour of cartoons Dad
raises his head like a trumpet's messenger
with a fabulous idea to build
a family room. It is hot. On the ride
to the lumber store my brother sits in
front next to Dad and I ride in the bed
of the pick-up—wind drinking my pale skin.
The lumber yard is filled with fresh sap, and boys
with no shirts, their bare chests like cedar bay.

Years later Ray forgets his own birthday
party. The room is now built and Mom
bakes a cake. "How could the Cartwrights behave
so kindly with a camera in their home?"
he wants to know. These are invisible
years; I barely know him. Once, off the roof,
without asking, Ray jumps into the pool,
and gets five swats from Dad. In this awful
room he runs away from a chair where his
photograph is being taken while Dad
is away for the weekend, like every
weekend, and he screams "I don't want Daddy
to see me." But one day he will want one
picture of his childhood. There will be none.

When Ray is twenty, the doctor tells him
that his liver will fail, he will die if
he does not stop drinking, but on a whim
he finds dark restaurants and bars and hits
the faces of gay men, getting even,

he thinks, with our dead Dad. He learns to hit
baseballs out of left and right fields. No one
can catch him. Young women, blondes and brunettes,
give him phone numbers. He does not want
to talk about his dad, or remember
the family room, and he does not want
to remember his brothers and sisters
who left him alone in the chair, who laughed
while he cried, while Mom held him down for Dad.

My Red Dress

Boy-like and raking carrots and green beans
into their own river dance in the garden
behind our house, I designed a red dress,

and still Mother would not let me read *Little Women*,
"Take it back," she said. "Don't bring those sinful
books home ever, ever again." All my life

I have walked down ice, though no one
could see my melting. I touched a swing set once
at Debbie's house where satin drapes

whispered to me. At my house, we beat our hands
on trees as if they were drums; we threw pine cones
toward each others' faces, across the fields

where cows ran away, and now I do not even speak
to my brothers. At times, though, my past gives way to
the day my brothers and I formed a team

of hitters. Other boys could only hope
to hit the balls we pitched. I guarded first base
and I tagged-out our neighbor, Steve, who swore

he was "safe" — so I called him motherfucker, bastard,
crybaby. I knew that someday I would leave that field
and make many dresses for my closet. After that I played

baseball only to hear boys scream when they lost,
I didn't know that hitting a hard ball would send all boys
home. I didn't know that if you ask a boy for blueberries

he will kiss you, so I put my face in the way of one man's
many losses. I did not know I would become
a woman who would give her only red dress to the first

man who demanded it. The dress I made
was too tight and too short, but my father liked it,
and now, my anger lives in a glass jar.

Wallpaper

Purple hills and green houses run
together in the wallpaper around my room. My daddy
runs his hands down, gliding over the cut

edges where they join with paste. The paste holds
down my tongue. *Do you like it?* I swallow so daddy's
princess can exist. Stare over hills into darkness
beyond green houses
where people live happily
where purple hills are not bruises
where little girls laugh. No daddy

loves his princess more; he buys wallpaper. Mommy
sees the edges peel, superglues them down so no one
sees. *It's silly to have wallpaper like that, why
did you ask for it anyway?* I did not
ask for it—I drop my head, close my eyes. Inside
my head crowds of people run away
with me to the other side of the room and wait
in the corner

under the window, ready to throw
our weightless bodies out in to the purple hills,
ready to stay away for a long time—all night
if we have to. Princess will know when it's time
to return. When daddy leaves her

alone again. When he tells her to forget.
It's important to be quiet. Do you like it?
nodaddynodaddyidont

Map of Charleston, West Virginia

Narrow streets, tight alleys, houses kissing, and vines
eating windows must have reminded my father
about his father coming home filthy from the mines,
taking him into the back room, pulling down
his pants, the blinds all the way down
to the floor, making my father, at nine years old, lie
on the floor beneath his naked body. And his mother
behind the wall, her knife against hard
wood, chopping beans in the kitchen. From the hill
where the governor lives on our only
visit to his hometown, my father showed me how you can see
the whole city from up there—the river, a dead black snake
running through town, separating the rich
from coal miners, the coal dust changing buildings
to black, and the smoke. He told me how the streets
of Charleston hold secrets, his hands trembling
on the steering wheel, and how inside
one of those caves that touches the side
of the road, he and three classmates hid the day
they skipped school, taking sacks
of bologna sandwiches and bottles of water. At the end
of the day they crawled out, stood
on ashened earth, looked in each other's eyes, and saw
that one of them was missing. I watched my father's face,
that day, trace the hours the other boy must have
crawled through endless
tunnels calling out his friends' names, lighting his last stolen
cigarette, drinking water alone, and finally resting. And his voice
seemed to stretch the days of the lost boy
into decades of his own secret
drinking, weekends away from home,
forgetting what he was responsible for. My father's voice longing,
not for his friend, I think,
but for a way to hide in a darkness like that.

[24]

An Ordinary Door

I was four and the preacher
had said, When you pray, enter into your closet,
and when you have shut the door,
pray to your Father in secret, so I let my father
into my closet, let him lift my dress and sing
in his money-
making tenor voice,
                    save this little
                              wretch, like me,
I knew that God saw everything I did,
so I crawled inside a suitcase
and shipped myself off.

For years, I pressed his voice
between forgotten pages of a hymnal,
finally cut him out of the family pictures.
But every year, on the anniversary of his death,
he quotes his scripture again
and again: *Behold I stand at the door*
and knock: if you hear my voice, and open
the door, I will come in to you.
And so I go to his grave site and say to him,
as in prayer, Father—as if
he can hear me—I have come here to take you,
twenty years dead, by the collar bone and shake you
until you beg me to stop. I listen to cemetery
silence, expecting the mockingbird to sing,
but the cry of a red-tailed hawk
drops into the pine scrub.

My life is the urn he lives in. I find
my way to the kitchen window. I see a yard in need
of grass seed and birdsong, and want to carry

myself over the aching earth. The well-trained wind
hollers, and I believe I will never hurt again. I believe I can
forbid my father from entering.

Holiday Gifts

Mother opens the curtains on her moon-drenched
calamondin tree behind the rock
garden out back. It is Christmas 1967. Or 1973.
She is standing in the forest of dreams,
holding a book—the Bible I'm certain—in which her ancestors
reveal the requirements of simple tea
and folding hands for God. Later my father rises
and goes out to milk the old cow. Inside the house

one of my brothers half-awakens, walks around
the foot of his bed,
lifts a pillow and pees. One by one the other five children
rise. We meet under the silver tree against
the glass doors. I open a box of hair pins.
        Then it is Christmas Eve 1990, Mother sits

in a chair at my brother's house, his wife and children
spinning around a tree she does not
recognize. Earlier that year, before her body
could not lift itself, she cross-
stitched a table cloth as a Christmas gift
for me, her oldest daughter. It is the holiday
she can not remember
my name.
        At the funeral in January, her mother
sits next to me—an old woman
whose first child is dead. My retarded brother opens
the doors of the church, walks the aisle,
presses his hand
and his oversized ear to Mother's coffin, whispers
her name. Years later, she will reveal herself to me

as bone, touching my cheek, her hands
cool and hard and clothed in scripture. But at her funeral,
behind me, there are dozens of Welsh relatives, hard

workers, pipelines in their bulging cheeks,
bowing their heads. Like Mother,
they've spent useless years learning to pray.

Proof

Across from my childhood house
beyond the ditch, in high grass,
wanting to carry in my hand a leaf
from the tree in the front yard
to prove that I lived
this place through,
I whisper, *I'm running away for good*
as I did when I was six. But now the window
of my old room upstairs brings me closer
to the road between me
and the swimming hole my father dug
in the backyard, like a dog,
crouched, looking for something
he could only smell. There are toys
that I lost, and the picture in my mind of the edge
of the bed where he sat, called me
princess, and told me to not tell
anyone — *they will know you are crazy,*
lock you up, throw away the key. This I know
because my mother found me
crouched behind his chair in the living room,
pretending to have run away. I played
for her on the piano:
> *Jesus loves me, this I know*
> > *For the Bible tells me so,*
> *Little ones to him belong,*
> > *They are weak, but he is strong.*

Then my father came home, and at daybreak
the robin cried: *Dear Jesus, I promise to say*
my prayers morning, noon, and night, even though
a little girl got lost here — poor little sinner.

Said the preacher every Sunday: *There is a war*
between God and Satan. God is
like your earth father, only bigger.

And now there are too many years,
like yesterday when a stranger in a deserted
coffee house wrote me a note in a foreign language.
It says I want you, he told me,
and then he put his hand,
tight, around my fist. I know what it is like
to be a stranger, but I wanted to hear
his version, so I told him
that in my dreams a man stands above a woman
with a gun, puts his fingers into her mouth
and grabs the memory she's always
wanted to be rid of. Blood
rushes from her mouth into the garden,
like the one Jesus prayed into.

The day I stayed home
sick from school, asleep in my
parents' bedroom, I heard Satan
shuffling things in the garage, and I wondered how
he got the key. I wanted to fly
like Jesus off the cross, because I knew his weight
would press me into bedspread
nubs that rubbed my neck, and of course
I knew he couldn't breathe
in daylight. I stood on the foot
of their bed, dared myself to fall
back, like death, stiff and solid, and hoped
Jesus would save me. But I had, like today, no leaf
in my hand; instead, I crossed my arms
over my chest, as if blessing myself
and leaned back.

Tent of Freaks

Today, on TV, a stranger spoke
of how her mother made a choice when the daughter
was five years old to amputate her
right leg, and I remembered the word of God
as it was told to me:
if your right hand deceives you,
cut it off. I have felt the earth
beneath both
my feet, yet all my life I have been a distortion
of female. At the fair
in my hometown, not wanting to peek
into the tent of freaks,
I wandered away

from that side
of the fairgrounds. In the house
of mirrors I saw myself fattened
and dwarfed. I refused the Ferris wheel, the men
who wanted to guess my birthday
or weight, their hands
on my jeans, the women with crystal balls
and incense. When the fair demanded
too much of my allowance I stopped going,
until a friend, who lived behind
the grounds, helped me climb the fence,
got me in for free. Still I did not want
my fortune told, did not want to see
the lines in my palms. I did not want
to know what I had left to lose.

My Mother, the Missionary

for my mother, Mary, 1927-1991

Jasmine bloomed, and Mother tried to remember
walking in woods behind her childhood house
picking honeysuckle, violets. She wanted,

in the last year of her life, to remember
the squirrels and rabbits, the birds, and the crickets,
even though, years before, she had given up

becoming a missionary. She married, instead,
a man who gave her thunder,
and a vacuum cleaner for five bedrooms,

a stove for cooking him sour dough bread,
hot guava jelly, six children. After he died,
she waited for the door to open into wind

through cotton woods, and then, in the last
year of her life, she wrote to her first daughter:
it might even rain...

if you are left behind. I remember you
shut your infant eyes so tight, and then cancer
swallowed her like a prayer

in a thin white tea cup. She had not imagined
a room blue and white and rain
outside a hospital. I am her first daughter.

Tomorrow, I must take my shovel to her grave,
pry open the lid of her coffin.
I must be careful not to wrinkle

the only dress she owned. I will buy two plane tickets,
order apple juice and peanuts, and use
all three seats. In New Guinea, I will steal a jeep,

drive past the towns, out into the unknown
villages, and climb to the mountaintop.
I will tell the natives to get down on their knees,

Mother's bones a clumsy wind chime in my arms.

Fourth of July

1970

In another war with my brother, I swing higher,
touching my toes to the switches hanging from trees.
The celebration lingers
in the leaves behind us where everyone is singing
in the churchyard, and my father,

in shorts and open-toed sandals, red and white striped
socks, stars on top, drunk (or dumb), pretends to be President of
Happy Children.

1980

Our jeep wanders in dirt past the city pier
to a field of sand and ferns. At home, my husband said that I was
    dragging
my twenty-year-old ass while I loaded jell-O,
fruit, hamburger, then wood for the fire, and so, with justice for all,
he grabbed my ear and dragged me into the jeep to celebrate.

1990

The calendar never stops reminding me of the men
I left behind. The church is gone, the liars are dead,
and the past takes bets on
how many years I will hum this tune.

III

Small Bending Hope

Dream Ride

Mom, next to me
in the back seat, ignores
me like a stupid
tea cup resting on

a table. I reach
over my brother, who is
driving, for the maps
hidden under his

seat, and while he laughs
at my arms crying
for direction,
I see that Mom's face

is marble smooth.
Her voice, a letter
never sent. Ahead of us,
a movie from the past

I don't recognize:
children laughing,
a woman burying
her face

in the boxes of food
packed in the back
of a station wagon,
a boy aiming a toy rifle

toward the woman,
and a man behind
the camera,
the woman's hand

waving him away.
In my hand
rattlesnake soup dances
and reminds me

that Mom's face
is not smooth, it is
a gravel driveway. I remember
the first time

I dropped a snake
into our swimming
pool. It wriggled toward
the bottom filter. There was

a woman shaking
her fist—Mom. Now my brother
keeps driving, then forgets
where to turn,

and the baseball of our childhood
enters the window
like an unarmed
message. From the edges

of the baseball, he pulls
out the thread
as he drives. Around
the corner he sees

bluebirds, and says
he wants to study
them and their sound,
this way he will understand

the silent words in the movie,
so he takes the road
to the left, and gets out,
hoping the bluebirds

will respond to
whatever it is he is
trying to say. And a little girl
in the backseat

is holding
her mother's face
as if she can bring her back
to life.

Scrub Jay's Voice

to my brother, Jon

You took us away
every afternoon from the static
that lived inside

our house. We marched behind
you into the pine forest
where you tied

your bandanna around
a tree trunk
so we could find our way back.

You knew everything:
when the sun would crawl
back into the earth

how little voices would appear
as mockingbirds that glanced
the other way, and then

there were summer vacations
when our father flew
from the driver's seat

like a mad fighting cock
waving his wings
threatening to take us

to the police station and leave us
there like orphans if we did not
shut up and let him drive goddamnit.

Our Mother spent years
bent over
the blistering oven

baking her bread
and now you want to name
a scrub jay refuge for her,

our mother who kept
whispering *some things just
make you homesick,*

our mother who called us
in for dinner. It was you
who, night after night, stumbling

and in secret, put our drunk
father to bed. I want to go back
to our pine forest.

Stand with you beneath
our trees. Hear your voice
teaching me the scrub jay's song.

I want to watch the tongues
of unrelenting saw palmetto
buried in the Florida sand.

But you taught me that trees
offer nothing except distance.

Tidal Wave

I swing out over the river
on a rope
and let my body find
its way into the brown
water as if I will never again
be happy. Clouds swell and water
cradles my body. My brother jumps
in beside me and we
drift to shore, and though
Mom has been dead
five years, she is drinking a cup
of tea; the bones of her fingers
brittle as they rise and fall. Always, when I dream

of home, I am falling into water
or running on a sandbar, and while other children
are calling for a parent,
I can not find my way home
where I would listen to Teeny Grandma
tell stories.

I see the past in her dead eye:
my mother on a horse
drinking rust-colored
water from the trough, my brother and me
walking to school, looking for empty
soda bottles, trading them for candy, stopping
at Teeny Grandma's house
to water her bonsai tree while Mom waits at home for us,
every morning and every night,
drinking her tea. But now a darkness
rises, and a swell of water from
below the sunset lifts itself into the sky,
and pulls me
toward deep water.

Mother's Necklace

I was the painted tongue, and when I called
her name that she had hidden beneath
terrazzo floors, dried flowers
called for morning, and I invited my son
to ride bikes with me into the woods where we walked
through high grass, through lichen,
toward a stream. Then Mother's necklace
called me home, and, in my dream, she was reading
the truth I had written, *Mother never played*
games with me. The voice of reason: if you bury
a necklace, it will come back as earlobes, but
I am in exile—Mother never wanted my
voice, even though I tried to tell her
I was not a white ballerina pretending
to be a flamingo. Last week there was an alligator
in my flowerbed—nine feet—the trapper
wrapped each pair of legs with electric tape,
taped his eyes shut. A man across the street
called the TV station—hungry, they said, for a
girlfriend, and my son sat on the sidewalk
and sketched the scales on his back. I did not want
to be reminded of the failure of my life: a dead
baby, three husbands, a dirty kitchen. Mother told me
I'd never keep a man because my bangs creep
into my eyes. Mother, I can see through my hair now,
I can see the box where I keep the necklace you did not
want to wear even in your death,
I can see you waving, giving birth to
a memory I don't want back—terrazzo beneath
my feet, a tree I once knew, the living
room chair I hid behind
so you'd think I'd finally escaped, so you would not put
a dust rag in my hand, you playing card games
without me, your teeth, firm,
staring at me, beads on my tongue.

Girls at Slumber Party

At slumber parties
we dipped sleeping fingers
into warm water,
collected and lit candles
in dark, crowded bathrooms,
tried on luscious red lipstick
and kissed the mirror
designing the perfect lip position,
dared to tell secrets,
picked straws for the cute boys,
drew pictures of what they looked like
under their fading blue jeans
(we knew that just thinking it
could make you pregnant),
we froze training bras
of those who fell asleep too soon,
asked the Ouija board
who we'd marry
and how many children we'd have,
brought magazines we found
in our parents' bedrooms,
under mattresses, behind night stands,
men and women
alive with dark lines,
drawn together as one long ocean,
we read ourselves
into the lovers
and held each page like wet paint.

How I Learned Romance

Aunt Peggy's house was full of romance
    novels, books for twelve-year-olds in the alcove,
        and while Mother kept her doctor's appointment
across the street, I sat on the brown sofa at my
    aunt's house where she read of gentle, strong bodied

men. After two or three red delicious apples, I took
    a book from the shelf and read of a boy
        with a terrible stomach ache, the pictures
in silhouettes. The doctor took the boy behind a curtain
    and on a long table laid him down. His shadow

peered into the boy's mouth. The words asked where it
    hurt. Bicycles, lamps, palm trees, and horses
        rose from the boy's body, and years
later, in her kitchen, Aunt Peggy's voice
    rose toward my mother who had come to take me home.

Girls who wear pantyhose are not
    whores, she said, and make-up is for girls who
        want to look nice, not loose — but my mother,
solid (as always), stepped closer to Aunt Peggy's
    face. *Not my daughter*, she said. Hoping.

Mary, said my aunt, *she's sixteen.* My aunt was a nurse
    and knew more than my mother about
        girls and boys, which is why, years later, when I
was nineteen, I took her my first born,
    miscarried, in a glass jar after my husband made me

keep it — his pride, my failure — for days. But at sixteen,
    every Saturday night before church on Sunday,
        I went to Aunt Peggy's house. Her two
daughters and I spent hours in the bathtub,
    smoothing our legs with shaving cream Aunt Peggy

had bought us—specially for women. We polished nails, curled hair,
      traded eye-shadow. My uncle, who threatened to cut us up
            with a chain saw each time he raised his head
from an engine in the dark shed in the backyard—drunk—
      sent us to bed because we were vain—

whores, he called us one Saturday night. From
      down the hall the springs of their bed creaked and his
            voice, startling the thick Florida air, crept
into the screen of our windows, seeped through our
      gowns, devouring our bodies. His voice saying

Shut up, Peggy, shut up. I'll kill you. My older
      cousin—the springs louder—left our room to
            save her mother. But it was his hand around
my cousin's wrist, his hand across her furious
      cheek that taught her the lesson, his voice that

echoed the hall's shadows. Then it was Aunt Peggy who
      grabbed his arm, phoned her mother, and sent us out
            into the street to wait, our flowered
cotton gowns around us, scarring the dark. All night
      we imagined what he might do to her. Imagine three girls

wanting to save Aunt Peggy. Imagine us on the window sill
      at our grandmother's house, lifting the hems of our gowns,
            leaping into the starry night, picking branches
off trees as we fly past them, our gowns
      like dust against leaves. Imagine us approach

the window of my aunt's bedroom, her delicate silhouette
      behind the curtain, my older cousin flies
            into the room, and, with the branches,
wraps her father's arms around the bedpost while my
      other cousin guards the foot of the bed. Imagine me

wipe the sweat and hair from her cheeks, and with the leaves
we brought, I adorn her hair. Imagine
the three of us as we hold hands, forming a circle
around Aunt Peggy. And, from one of her romance novels,
we read the words to her.

Cow Skulls

Out of sunset, beyond home plate,
the moon rose, and our mother's voice, wavering,
called us home. Jon, my big brother, carried a new snake
from the trail of flattened
pine needles and dry grasses. We passed the chicken
shed where we had built a lookout
in the rafters, crossed our home-made
ball field where he had complained to the outfield
about his two athletic brothers
who always hit home runs. Jon fed
small peanuts to scrub jays, and at night
he lay in bed, thin and smelling of pine, his new
indigo snake beside him. He dreamt
about birds, until his face —
open like the sky and worn by the simple
fascination of a bird's egg — crumbled
into the nightmare:
driving to stop our father from another drink,
thinking of home, behind him the woods,
driving, under the reckless hope
of trying to save us all;
driving, sick for the warm
kiss of a scrub jay, for blackberries
growing without a fence
to lean on, for the trails, where
bones and skulls of dead cows
stared into long pines and dead brown grass.

Furious Arrow

When I was young
I noticed the children next door asking a robin
to teach them the songs
of trees. Later, I gave birth to a boy
and he unwrapped the sky. Now I walk to the window
behind the vase with tulips and watch
dawn try to tear apart
the dark, but the tulips grow
tired waiting for sunlight. And I think,
here is a woman exhausted
at thirty-seven, destined
to lean on the furious arrow
that demands women stand up
for themselves. How will I find the road to forty?
Sometimes at night, walking home, I hear
bells down the street,
and I know that one day
even my son will leave,
and sometimes my mother calls
from her death asking to see
the quilt she made. Then she shows me
our old house, moves
furniture around, tears down the walls
between my room and my brother's,
and gives me more furniture, but I have
nowhere to put it. One night my lover
whispers into my ear that I am
a sweet woman, easy to love,
says the first time he touched me
he knew he loved me. Then one day
a younger man shows me—
and because I'm almost forty I want to see it—
his journal, tells me he's enamored with me.
When a friend shows me a mirror
sculpted with pink flowers, I tell her that in it I see aging.

She says, no, what you see
is fear. I want to dream myself with wildflower
hair and my lover a waterfall
from the north cooling the Florida sun.
What if my family forgets me?
What if my lover dies before me?
What if I stand on the roof of my house
and notice that all housetops look the same
under a full moon?
What if the sun appears desperate, what if all these things
that have happened to me are connected?
What if the trees say nothing.

Forgotten Morning

Weeds, deer flies, and empty buck shot,
like a constant family, attach themselves to my hands, ears,
eyes, and clothing, while a peewee calls, *See-a me?*

I wear a hat and a fawn slips across the trail.
Sheets of wildflowers.
Trees commanded by wind. To be still. To move.

Along the marsh the trail reads my feet
as tall, weighted grass, but I have left my friend's siblings
behind who, unlike my brothers and sister, are drawn toward

one another, toward their mother's house — its
front yard of bird feeders,
lawn chairs, basketball hoop, and tended wildflowers,

its weekly dinners, as if each sibling
were an abandoned cornfield needing seed after years of want.
Its laughter.

Pine weighs on my tongue. And mud, like rotted oak and fish.
Still the remote peewee calls as though
he is lonely as an orphan. *See-a me?* he asks, inviting me to

talk. *See-a me?* I pull off my hat, raise
my binoculars, and the sky offers its philanthropy
all day. I tell the sky

of my dead parents, my brothers and my sister who live
far away, and the forgotten morning
moves, casting shadow on the cliff I must

walk up to reach the bottom of the trail. One day birds
will call me by name. I will go to them.
For now, I say back to the peewee, *I hear you, but can't*

see you. Do you see me? I hold tight to what I have—
a wild turkey feather and a hollow carapace that once,
to a box turtle, was home.

Small Bending Hope

Wanting to be held, I walk into the idea
of my mother where, tucked beneath her blue dress,
is talk of romance, the sky, and my father—

the drug addict dead at fifty-three.
Always it had been the silence
that I hated, but now, I welcome the past

I tried not to remember:
lying in a silent room with flowers
brought by mourners who wished me alive,

the light in the hallway going on
and on. And though I hold my past
in a galvanized bucket, behind the branches

there is darkness gathering like steam.
My past has been hidden by years
with no scent. Was it not me falling into

the stagnant pond, the emptiness of it
leaking from my hands? Here, where my
parents' voices now live, even the darkness

disappears just behind the cinder blocks
my father once used to close in the family
room. If I am to be comforted I must not look

toward the sky, for I will find myself
wishing I were a crow, wishing for those nights
when I did not know my past. I am a person

whose windows might fill with slivers of loneliness,
a person who might give away
all the stories she owns, a person who once

wished away her parents' deaths.
There is a past I pretend to believe in,
and a small bending

hope that in someone else's hands I will find myself,
lying outside the barren forest,
beneath the silent scoop of moonlight.

IV

Water Letting Go of Sunlight

Absence of Water

1

From a prairie of white egrets
a woodstork rises
and for a moment
I forget that the sun
has lamented
its own ascent all day.

Somewhere north
of a red-wing singing
o-ka-lee (come love me)
a plane lands
safe, I think

but the fishcrows are crying
trying to find their way to shore
with too much wind on the water.

2

I fix clouds for breakfast
and outside two white egrets
circle the lake.
I think of how I want
to be born again
inside this flowered dress.

Then out of the dove-gray sky
one egret returns to shore
leaving a desperate shade of water
on the grass. I think of how his mate quivers
across the lake, how a tree splits
and how the daisies are now separated petals
in a crystal bowl.

3

I am ready to be pagan again,
become caracara
the wild long-legged
long-necked hawk
of my native prairie.

How is it I want so many things—
the woodstork and the caracara,
the sunset and the sunrise
and in the absence of water
want to touch the color of the sky
and a tangled field of deer-tongue
and pinweed and marchello.

The sky is a faint click of small words
and has its own desperate language.
Hunger will bring the woodstork back.
Tomorrow will come

but like wildflowers once given to me
a door must first be opened.
The moon undresses the lake.

The Fairy Tale

The arm of a man—when the woman eats
petals so carefully from a daisy they seem to turn
into rough wool—is pine, but the woman needs

more petals than the daisies can give
and the night widens

and the woman and the man go on
needing the white and the rain.

She brings the daisies inside
plants them in a whining bucket, strands

grow, yellow clinging onto them.
Then the daisies begin to speak: *We are*
the museum of the woman you think you are.

She dreams of what it would be like
if the man takes his arm
into a forest and loves trees.

The daisies become wind in the corners of her house.

In the forest the man and a pine tree conspire.

The woman hires the tree to water the daisies
Hindsight is a cloud, she tells the man, and they sit down
at the table of daisies and nightmares, and the woman drinks

to morning and lifts her arm to the trees.

Find the River

Perhaps I even want snow
here, where icicles never fall

where sometimes the lights are on
for a few hours each day.

Empty puddles. No ice
on the pond.

Take the dark of my mouth

the ghost that comforts me.
Wait for water. A woman

paddles long to find love
or a life gliding just outside her back door.

The Bag Lady

The sky sags like an old woman collecting
sacks of men. Creeping past each other, the clouds
have lost hope, and yet the palmettos, flags
of surrender, rise this morning. Still,
it's hard to ignore the birds as they splash
in the bird bath, and the jasmine trying
to bloom. For love, a young woman
once rode out of this town that had taken
her money and given her too few men;
still, she thought the smooth sky of her life
would reach into a lake edged with cattails
and someday there would be a dirt road
and dinner with old friends, and sleep
would be only a brief announcement. Now
she knows that love only lasts so long
before it asks to be made into forever,
but then, again, old women have waited
their entire lives to leap from trees.

Another Night in Jealous, U.S.A.

There is a woman in a bed where sleep
does not exist. This dream will end behind
her lips gesturing desire. First she breathes
his name, in fragments, her arms and words fly
from her body. Oh, why do dreams obey
obsession? I see that this is her hand,
commanding him to worship. There is a
quarter under her words and her next chant
begins. Under her tossed hair, her fingers
singing, is dinner for two. In the room
she hangs his shirt opposite the mirror.
There are raw eggs, candle light, some
dancing. Then a song: fountains stop their wish
and she carries him across her loneliness.

He unbuttons his shirt, her dress; a fire
mounts in the building behind them, and songs
ride waves of cliché blue. Time mistakes my
tears for night. I'm chewing my dress, a bomb
talking. I want to run her out of town,
and then I want him to find angry rocks
in her language. Instead, they slither down
the pavement of my body and stroke
each other's lips. My toes are furious.
My hair is a shroud on streetlights. The chimes
insist that I feign madness. Then my dress
unwinds, the street turns on its side. Sometimes
I turn away, see nothing, and they laugh;
then she turns her head and I see myself.

The Comfort of Your Hands After Rain

At first I could not hold all the bird songs
you gave to me, and now those old myths

grow farther away, those ancient birds

where I would have died if
I'd been asked; years ago you took me through

a swamp, we thought that one day
the path might merely become

rotted wood; instead it became

this branch and the vireo. I take his song
into my hands, and still our walking puzzles the grass,

where old graves of turtles, snakes,
last year's birds wait for each morning,

only to feel the dew above them.

Past the swamp, in an unfamiliar dark forest
we lie down, the child in me

standing in the distance as if
she is watching a foreign film

and she hears thirty years fly past her
in the whip-poor-will's voice:
poor, poor girl,

> *poor, poor girl,*

but then she forgets who she is, and reaches
into the movie, and asks me,
> "Where is the lake?"

And I remind her, as I do
every night, that we must listen to your voice,

we must feel your hands,
consoling our body with leaves,
rainwater, daisies,
                    and the wet earth beneath us.

Woman Reading at River

Late morning. A pair of red-shouldered hawks
abandon the tall branches of long pines, and I look up

from the pages I have come to wade through
in peace. Wind on water becomes words

bobbing across a page. Quiet. Dragonfly. Sleep.
A yellowlegs hammers out words

in water as if it is a sheet of paper where I have written
all my love songs.

Mosquitoes scribble on my arm.
From the waterlilies, a duck neglects the silence of herons

who seem embarrassed and lift themselves
from sound. Across the river a house wades through

woods, barely visible, then departs. A red-wing blackbird
calls his mate, *home love-ly?* and reminds me

that I want to live here, on this water, with him,
where everything is silent except when needing

territory or food. But beyond the hammocks
of oak and palm, a child waits for me. A city

hides this silence.
And a man lives in my hands.

Ovarian Cyst

An hour before my surgery you quizzed me
about a Celtics game, how Bird shot one
from behind the basket—*did it count?*
you asked—you're my lover girl, you kept saying,
touching my hair, then—*what's an over-and-back?*
I answered one of them right.

The anesthesiologist told you
she'll forget you kissed her
and I did.
I woke up looking at the clock:
8:40 in a room with one long metal table, tubes
hanging from walls, a little light, two nurses.
Someone wanted a break. Another patient whose ovaries
had been removed, moaning, and I was the lucky one,
only the cyst. Someone asked
my name again.

I returned to my room and the clock,
broken, read 8:20. You handed me flowers
in a sailboat cup—I could've floated
out of there but I could not wake up
you told me at eleven
I could stay at the hospital all night,
told me you'd come back at nine in the morning—
all night I waited 40 minutes: the light
in the hall, nurses forgetting to kill
the pain, door left opened, the clock reading
8:20. Voices of women and men, light,
nurse, thermometer my mouth.

In the morning the doctor showed us
pictures of the laparoscopy: a mass
of blood and tissue, cyst
big as an orange, bleeding into the abdomen,

the fallopian tubes, the ovary, the uterus,
and something, she said,
that was supposed to be white. The day before
as they prepared me
for surgery, so that I would forget the pain held inside
my body, you had asked me to tell you
stories of a boring television show over and
over—*General Hospital*, something I'd watched
for twenty years. I told you that before I learned to trust you,
its characters were the people I counted on,
and created stability in my life. The nice gangster
who refuses to use physical force and marries
the wrong girl to save himself from a life
in prison, the psychopath who in prison befriends
the craft woman who helps him escape. Gives him a drug
to lower his heart rate, so he appears
dead. She arranges a funeral,
buries him, then when the time is right, she digs him
up, and as he is thanking her,
holding her gently from behind, he wraps
a thin white rope around her neck
and kisses her goodbye.

Everglades

At the edge of sawgrass prairie we're hoping for deer
and the bending gate of pines.

We've stolen this weekend, then
a meadowlark calls. We wait,

but we can't find him in our binoculars.
Then, he calls again.
Somewhere
            above us. Will we ever find
his yellow wagon?

Back at the hotel, we forget the years
behind us:

when we opened suitcases
filled with banquets of smiles that we hauled

from separate lives. I'm her, I keep telling myself,
and during the night, the meadowlark totes his greeting
to a tree above us, then
warblers,
        vireos,
                woodpeckers fill up

the room, become angels,

and the next day when we're back in the woods,
walking a road that no one has considered for years,

lost in the damp kettle of sawgrass…

Wind Through Blackbird Wings

Econlockhatchee River State Forest, October 19, 1996

The oak drops brown notes into the river,
      and from the stories of my childhood,
            I hand you Florida sand. The promise
      of my body among roots of flatwoods.
Daylight pours into the river. A canoe

clutters air. Pine needles. No blue jays.
      But if goldenrod could fly, it would leave
            this place and travel north, taking its thin
      root, its yellow-orange that sweeps this sky.
We cross the river and you make me laugh,

and I wonder what you do when we're not
      together. If you die before me, I will carve
            your name in this tree. Night will begin here,
      in my hair as when it fell into your cupped
hands. I will leave this river. At the marsh

I will walk beyond the stream that once
      separated us from shorebirds. I will whisper
            your name, plovers and dunlins and sandpipers
      will lift their heads hoping for your call,
I will run among them, they will rise

from water in mourning swaying their high songs
      against the sky. I will cry your name across
            the grasses. You will come back to me, a scent
      gathering oak, spartina, black needlerush,
leather ferns. I will hold branches instead

of your hands. Goldenrod. Walking with you
      will be wind through blackbird wings.
            The sun will throw its mango orange
                  into the field. I will be a woman alone.

Invisible Birds

I am trying to recall my walk this evening,
if I took one, if the wave of sky
at the corner of the street brought me
home, and I am trying to remind
myself that my lover is in the next room
reading a book without me—I am almost certain
that he once showed me the words
of wilderness, and if I could crawl into the trunk
in the corner, I might find an explanation of
my invisible life—perhaps the dinosaur my son drew,
or the photograph of myself at ten
in a swimsuit, wet, arms at my stiff side
—a ten-year-old marine prepared to obey
her daddy's orders. I have already forgotten
all the birds my lover gave to me in the shallow water,
and I do not recall when I hung
the burlap on my wall or if I am the one
who hammered the nail. There is no scented candle
next to the feathers in the crystal vase,
but somewhere llamas watched the sunrise
and someone bathed in the river of brown
and gray. There are no peaches in the basket
near the duck who could, if he really wanted to,
find a pen or an envelope and ask
a friend to save him. There are no more
beaded birds upon my cheeks.
There is no longer a clock in my fingers.
There is no man in the next room with lust
for my slender arms. There is no mailbox
on a street lined with oaks,
there is not even this room and I do not know
if I am in the book my lover reads or if
I am only the shadow from a dream I once had
in which palmetto fronds swayed above us
and a few small birds I could not name.

Water Letting Go of Sunlight

At the marsh without me you listen
to sandpipers sewing their beaks
onto the mudflats and you are remembering
last week when you drove
along the marsh trail and I sat on top
of the car and sparrows appeared from beneath
my hands they rose from wax myrtle
on the trail's edge near the water in the dark wind after
we had driven a deserted trail
for hours and found the locked
gate where a mammal slid into leather
ferns and above us a tower of vultures laughed at our
misfortune and we turned
the car around on our way back dusk
slipped into my hat the snow geese were
invisible and I opened
my mouth to the shallow light and the mudflats became
blood for the coots clustering together
for warmth even though they see nothing beyond
the flow of black feathers and when we
stopped I found a broken wing on the path
in front of the car I touched it
first then you wrapped it in a rag I thought of how
much we keep inside ourselves but just then the water
let go of the sunlight and I turned
to face you at the edge of the trail you were
leaning against the sunset I saw your mouth
round like an O how I want now to taste the spartina
grass as I try to imagine you are
now where nothing comes between
trees or grass where nothing not even the marsh
not even you let go of my body

Lightning Source UK Ltd.
Milton Keynes UK
UKOW041222070513

210300UK00002B/17/P

9 781844 715114